DREAMING WITH BIRCH

A Tree Spirit Short Read

Heather Sanderson

Majestic Wisdom Publishing

Copyright © 2021 Heather Sanderson

DREAMING WITH BIRCH
A Tree Spirit Short Read

Majestic Wisdom Publishing
www.majesticwisdompublishing.com

All rights reserved.

This book is not intended as a substitute for the medical advice of physicians or psychologists. The reader should regularly consult a physician or psychologist in matters relating to his/her/their health and particularly with respect to any symptoms that may require diagnosis or medical attention.

Cover image by Marina Pershina on www.publicdomainpictures.net. This image has been zoomed in and cropped.
Editing by Deanna McFadden

ISBN: 9798533815161

CONTENTS

Title Page
Copyright
Introduction ... 1
Tree Consciousness ... 5
What is a Tree Spirit? ... 9
What Does it Mean to Dream with a Tree? ... 10
How to Dream with Birch ... 12
The Spirit of Birch ... 20
Overview of Birch Medicine ... 24
Birch Folklore ... 29
Journey into the Dream with Birch ... 35
A Bonus Benefit ... 40
Over to You ... 42
Acknowledgements ... 44
Endnotes ... 46
About the Author ... 47

Books by this Author......48

INTRODUCTION

Every spring and summer as a child, I spent many days nestled in the Birch growing beside our house. The Y-shaped trunk of this particular tree was just low enough for me to step up into—a proper foothold. From there, I climbed onto one of her main branches that swooped out to the side at the perfect arc to hold my body, laid back, and read. As I read page after page, book after book, with Birch, our relationship grew into companionship.

I climbed many other kinds of trees, too. The Maple in the front yard was where I hid during Hide and Seek (because no one ever looked up); the Poplar in the back was for adventure, as I climbed high into her branches and felt as if I could fly; the Cherry tree was for stalwart curiosity; the Spruce became my fortress. But I only ever read with Birch. In a way, Birch was reading those same books too. Our energy and consciousness merged.

Spending time together and merging with Birch felt so natural that I didn't think much of it. Birch was my friend. I would climb up into her supportive branches when I wanted to be held, hugged. Resting there, feeling the just right curve of her solidness beneath me, I felt comfortable with my emotions, whatever they were. Much more comfortable than I felt showing them to humans, and Birch laid witness by accepting my emotional being in ways others couldn't. Ways I couldn't accept myself.

Most of the time, though, I felt completely content, lazing in body while my mind became filled with new places, characters, stories, and understanding of worlds other than mine from the books we read. From the outside, it might look like we were doing nothing at all; however, in these formative years, Birch provided a safe space to learn, be open to new ideas, to dream, and to innovate.

This particular Birch, the reading tree, grew with two others each about ten feet apart, to the northeast of our house, and I always thought of them as sisters. Another cluster of three Birch, planted to grow together as one, stood to the south, and one more trio to the northwest. Three sets of three trees made a triangle right around the center of our house. With my mind's eye, I saw then, and can still see now, the white and yellow lines of energy running between them, connecting and forming a web. An energetic way that they communicate, share, and also protect one another, creating a boundary of protection around the house, too.

What I didn't know then was that Birch is considered a trailblazer. As one of the first first trees to emerge after the last Ice Age, she is a seeker who explores the world through her being. The first to step onto the planet with her physical presence, as if emerging from the dream or consciousness of the Earth herself, Birch created a safe, inhabitable environment so that she and other plants, insects, animals, and people could not only survive, but thrive. I like to think that once her first evolutionary task of populating the Earth with her presence was complete, she still quested to have more understanding of this place, more ways to access the world.

Through the stories we read, perhaps Birch gained insight into different human experiences and ways of being in the world. Then, shared this information with her network of trees and the collective consciousness we all share. Birch had access to my consciousness as well as the active imagination and dream worlds within the pages of each book, and mind of each writer. She cultivated me into a dreamer, and made the idea of existing in many worlds at once feel normal and safe.

Constantly questioning and questing for more, Birch encourages you to explore places and stories, to innovate, to break new ground both internally in your emotional world and psyche, and externally in the world around you. Birch will hold you and keep you safe while you work through the trial and error that comes with living, especially with new ventures, will help you feel all the emotions that are inherent to growth, and will show you how to exist in many places at once.

TREE CONSCIOUSNESS

What does it mean to talk with or connect with trees? More so, why would anyone want to? To work with trees means that you need a foundation of understanding that they are conscious beings. In general, you might think of consciousness as awareness or a field of "something" of which we are all a part. It's that intangible source or energy that helps shape every aspect of our being and behavior.

Once you are able to see a tree as a conscious and living being you can then understand more of their intelligence. Plants and trees are our ancestors, and they have been here on Earth a lot longer than humans. They have evolved physically over a great deal of time in order to adapt and thrive as environmental conditions change. This information is stored in their consciousness, displayed physically in their forms and in their behavior. If left untouched by humans, trees unite in a canopy that bends and sways in the wind, working together like a big set of lungs. Beyond their unique ability to convert carbon dioxide into oxygen, trees perform a lot of other invisible work. Trees are connected to the Earth through their roots and our Cosmos through their branches with their trunk running information back and forth between the two, and many transmit information not only to other trees but to a larger energetic field that exists beyond Earth. Think of trees as guardians and gatekeepers who can show us the way into the "so below" and the "as above"—the realms of consciousness to which they constantly connect.

By dreaming with a tree, you are able to access or share in their consciousness, to receive information, and possibly even instruction. Often this has to do with spiritual, psychological, emotional or physical healing—and it can also be more tactile like being given a task to do. Since the work of trees spans from the Earth to the Cosmos, you may also discover messages that come through about our shared collective consciousness or even planetary information. Not even the sky is the limit.

For example, I always see a golden glow emanating around Birch, even before her leaves turn from green to yellow in the fall. While this energetic glow is generated through Birch, she selflessly shares it with me as I sit with her, in her branches, or nearby. As the energy enters my body, it has a subtle vibration, and, within a few moments, I have more of a glow too. Simultaneously connected and uplifted, thanks to Birch, I feel renewed, refreshed, and vibrant. In this way, Birch helps me understand how to be generative and generous so that my glow can spark a glow in those around me.

The information you receive may not be healing in nature. It may have to do with creating something —a piece of art for example or a different way of living. It could be a direct action that needs to happen. You don't need to work just with Birch for this, it can be any plant or tree. For example, I met a magnificent 800-year-old Oak tree in Ireland. After spending some time in her presence, I closed my eyes and asked if there was anything I could do for her. The Oak tree asked me to clean up the trash around her trunk (I heard these words appear out of nowhere and saw an image of her trunk). When I went to do so I found a used diaper that someone had stashed inside a hole in the bottom of her trunk. When removing the diaper, I felt flooded with gratitude at being able to do so. It was something that was so simple to do but I never would have looked there if I hadn't been shown what was needed. You can see with this clear example, any work you do with any plant, whether or not it's Birch, is possible and will be beneficial in some way.

People in many cultures, though not all, have forgotten that the plant, animal, and human worlds are not separate. Humans tend to separate and then believe in dominance or power over the other worlds. Again, not all humans do this, I'm speaking generally here and also from experience. When a person enters into the dream (or consciousness) of a tree or other plant it is there that the worlds of both become united and equal. It is with attention that we can then start to co-create with the plant world. If you think of the example of the Oak tree and imagine that its consciousness was talking to mine in some way, you can discern that the tree has no arms or legs but could ask me to do something on its behalf. Imagine if all humans were connecting with and listening to plants in this way and what we could achieve together.

WHAT IS A TREE SPIRIT?

The concept of a tree spirit is difficult to put into words because it can be experienced in so many different ways. To me, tree spirits are the consciousness and essence of a tree—that which is embodied in its physical form and exists around and outside of the physical body as energy and/or vibration. The spirit of a tree may also exist without a physical presence.

Think of your own spirit. What does the word spirit mean for you? Maybe you think of spirit as that energy or quality that animates your body, a vibration in your heart, the part of you that connects to some larger energy or life force. Beyond the energy of the physical tree, the spirit has the ability to move and be moved and to communicate in many ways that we can see, hear, feel or sense in some way, and often ignore. Dreaming with a tree is important because you can gain a sense of connection with what spirit means for you.

WHAT DOES IT MEAN TO DREAM WITH A TREE?

Dreaming with a tree can mean many things. Think of when you are asleep and dream, when you are able to connect with another plane of consciousness without much effort. If you try to remember your nighttime dreams, and work with them, there is always information to aid in your healing and wholeness. There is always information that you can bring back from that "other" non-physical world of the dream into your physical world. To dream with a tree means to share in consciousness or that dream place. Instead of entering it passively, as you would when asleep, you choose to enter this other world, pay attention to what comes, and then bring information back with you. You might consider this as active imagination or deep listening.

Often this means entering your own dream state or altered state of consciousness where you can be both awake and asleep. In that dream state, you are open to receive information in a different way. The rational mind isn't completely gone, but it's not as vocal as it can be, and these dream-like qualities can reveal other kinds of information.

Contrary to many beliefs, this does not require any mind-altering or hallucinogenic substances. In my experience this is a natural exchange of energy and information between humans and plants. It's an innate ability that we all have within us (before we learned how to be separate). This might be a challenging concept for some so we'll next talk more specifically about how to enter this dream state, what to do there, and why it's important.

HOW TO DREAM
WITH BIRCH

As you develop or deepen your relationship with a tree, there are key steps you can take to enter and work in the dream world. Some are concrete and more practical, and others require you to use your imagination and intuition. If you want a relationship with Birch, a helpful first step is to go and spend time with the physical tree. To do that, you might first need to identify Birch and if she grows near you. There are at least sixty varieties of Birch in both shrub and tree form and you can connect with any of them. Their bark and leaves range in color as does their stature, and their energy and spirit varies too, though they do hold some familial similarities. Here we'll focus mainly on Silver Birch, Betula pendula, sometimes also called European White Birch, especially in North America.

Silver Birch first originated in Europe and Asia, where she reaches from Siberia to China, to the mountains of Turkey and northern Iran, as well as central Europe to the United Kingdom. Humans brought her to North America as well as to the temperate regions of Australia. If she doesn't grow near you, don't worry. We'll talk later about other ways to connect with her energy.

Silver Birch is a deciduous tree that typically grows between forty-nine and eighty-two feet tall. Her trunk is covered in white bark flecked with black spots, which peels away and looks and feels like parchment or paper and is peach-colored underneath. As the tree ages, her bark starts to look silver, especially close to the ground. Silver Birch takes on different shapes as some grow tall and straight, while others are short and wide. Either way, she has slender, dark brown twigs that grow from her main paper-wrapped drooping branches and carry her flowers and leaves.

Birch flowers are called catkins. Male catkins appear in the winter and flower in the spring. They look like dangling clusters of rust-colored caterpillars, grouped in threes, and hold all of the pollen. Females grow in the spring and point upward as a single green catkin or cone, holding all of the seeds. The two meet on the wind and are easily scattered to generate new trees. Her pointed, triangular leaves have jagged or serrated edges, are bright green in the spring and summer, and turn a vibrant yellow in the fall.

Once you have identified Birch, or you are called to her intuitively, it's a good practice to ask permission from the tree before any encounter. You can enter a full-grown tree's energy field up to fifty feet away. Keep this in mind as you approach and see when you begin to feel the tree. It can help to have your hands by your sides with your palms facing the tree. You might sense or notice the edge of her energy field. As you approach you can ask in your mind or with a thought intended for Birch, "is it okay for me to connect with you?" Once you feel a sense of "yes," then slowly step closer to Birch. You might stand or lay down and look up at her branches, spend time with her flowers, sit with your back to her trunk, or place your forehead on her trunk. If you aren't sure what it means to "feel a sense of yes" that's okay—you might hear the word "yes," or get a feeling that all is well, or your head might even start to nod. However your own intuition guides you towards consent.

Once you feel connected with the tree, you can stay where you are or move around and start to study her with a soft gaze. Look closely at her trunk and where she connects with the earth. Imagine her roots below. Is she standing on her own, growing in a forest with other trees, or planted in a group with others? Feel the texture of her bark with your hand. If her catkins are present and within reach, touch them gently. Place your hand on her leaves or look up into her sweeping branches. Notice shapes, colors, and movement. Smell her scent. Birch's inner bark, leaves, and catkins are safe to eat, so you might place some in your mouth and notice her taste. The more sensory organs you involve in this meeting the better. This is something that you can take your time with and really get to know the tree.

You might consider drawing her to further deepen your connection. This might be your entire encounter and, whether you are aware of it or not, in this exchange you are already working on many levels with Birch. The joy of being in company of a tree friend is beneficial for both you and the tree. In my experience, trees tend to like the attention.

If you want to explore other connections with Birch, to go deeper into a dream state and into the world of the plants, there are several ways to do so. One way to do this is often called merging but you may hear other names such as entering an altered state of consciousness, shamanic journey, or active imagination. This is where you start to form a connection with the less physical aspects of the plant like her energy, consciousness, or spirit.

Some people try to sense the energy field of the tree. With Birch, for instance, you might walk to stand away from the tree and then approach slowly. Notice what you feel. What is the quality of the sensation in your body or around you? You can also place your hands gently on her trunk see what you notice. Close your eyes to help feel and imagine more. If you have trouble feeling something that's okay and if you don't believe there's anything there, that's okay too. If you try, you might be surprised by what you can feel even if it's invisible to you. If you'd like, you can think of bubble of energy or light around Birch that helps contain her and keep her healthy. You might also imagine or see energy running like a current through her trunk, separating down into the ground in two wide loops, each circling back up to join at the crown of the tree like a figure of eight. Some people like to see or imagine a being or energy that lives with the tree and helps her thrive. These beings are sometimes called Elementals or Devas, though they have many names. You can also think of this as an aspect of the energy and/or spirit of the tree as well.

Next, it's often helpful to close your eyes and start to imagine you are Birch. You become her. This process is where you merge with the tree. This is where, if you want to, you can think of it as using your active imagination. Here you may experience seeing visions, feeling sensations in your body, hearing sounds, or being moved physically in ways that are unusual for you. It is also possible that nothing much will happen, especially the first time. Using your active imagination works like a muscle and if it feels a bit rusty, keep trying. Trees are extremely patient teachers so there's no pressure to get something right or have it look or be a certain way. With trees, it's helpful to sit with your back against the trunk or place your third eye (located at the center of your forehead) on her trunk in order to help merge.

Once you can feel or see yourself as Birch, imagine

what it's like to be her. You might imagine what her trunk feels like as if you're on the inside of the tree. What qualities do you notice? What does it feel like to have your roots spread in the ground? To feel your branches move in the wind or get wet in the rain or snow? Imagine what it's like to witness the seasons change or stay present with what is happening right now. Can you feel what it feels like when your bark peels off? How does it feel to connect with the other trees or creatures nearby? It's helpful to fill in as many details as possible. It can be useful to draw or write down some notes as well. This might feel like enough, and you can do this as often as you and Birch want to.

As you merge and imagine, you are going deeper into the dream or consciousness of the tree. You might feel a desire to move, dance, sing, or you might see images or a story. If you are someone who sees images, one way to work with what is coming through from Birch is to draw or paint in an abstract way whatever you are shown. This is interesting to do as a group. To do this several people sit with Birch at a distance from one another or with their backs to the tree not looking at what the others are drawing. Usually, once everyone is finished and shares their work you will see common images, themes, and colors that have come through. The group's consciousness has joined together and merged with the tree's consciousness—and now you have visual proof. This also helps with confirmation if you feel skeptical or doubtful in any way—plus, it's fun to do!

As you can see there are a lot of options to experience connection with the less physical aspects of a tree. Once you have established a connection in a way that works best for you, you can ask a question of Birch. Maybe it's a question to do with your life or something you need help with. Perhaps it's a question for her. Whatever it is, hold it in your mind and, while staying in a merged state, see what answer comes. It might be an image or word. A sentence or two. Again, you might move or dance or hear sounds. You might feel vibrations that aren't "yours" and discern what it means when you sense another energy. There are only right answers and so the more open you are to any perception, the more answers you will receive. It's helpful to write down or record whatever comes.

You can then ask if there's anything Birch needs from you. Wait to receive an answer and then, if it's something you can agree to, do so and be sure to follow through with the request. Again, writing it down helps. Asking if there's anything you can do helps keep things reciprocal and helps restore an even balance of power between plant and human worlds.

Lastly, give thanks in some way—by expressing gratitude or giving an offering of some sort. This might be a physical offering like a bit of lavender, cornmeal, or another plant that wants to be offered, or it could be a song or dance. Some way of giving back and giving thanks for all that has been shared.

Once you feel complete, it's important to return fully from this experiential place. To come back from this journey or dream you deepen your breath, place your hands on the earth and move your body. Bending your knees if you're standing helps to stay connected and also brings you back to everyday awareness.

THE SPIRIT OF BIRCH

Now that you've explored merging with Birch, let's look at some of her attributes and what they might indicate on a psychological or spiritual level. These may be different than your own personal encounters and that's okay because your information and intuition matter the most.

Birch's spirit is one of initiation and leadership. Birch grows quickly, lives a short life span (as far as trees are concerned) of up to 150 years, with most living for 60 to 90 years. When she dies and falls, her soft wood breaks down quickly to give rise to other plant life. At night, her white bark glows and illuminates the area around her, lighting the way for those who pass through. One of the first trees to grow whenever there is environmental devastation or clearing of land by fire or other means, Birch instigates and, through her proliferation, leads the way for others to not only follow but to have what they need to thrive in their own right.

As she strikes out into the unknown, Birch is a seeker, knowledge worker, and communicator engaged in a constant evolutionary process. Imagine Birch, eager to get out into the world, planting herself, consuming or taking in all of the information around her, then feeding that information back into the web of life. Birch populates a repository of knowledge, sharing it with any who wish to connect. Some may call this a collective consciousness. While Birch is not the only contributor, she is a guardian of this collection and helps you to access it as well.

Keeping and sharing knowledge is one of the ways Birch is responsible for communication. It's as though she has energetic whisperings that help all species learn more about what needs to happen for the evolution of the planet, and Birch delights in leading in this way. Even her bark shows her natural aptitude for communication as it looks like, and has been used as paper. In many lands, Birch was the first to be written upon, bringing humans and plants together through written language and revolutionizing how communication happened—another evolutionary step.

As one of the first physical beings on the planet, and her aptitude for bringing life to barren or devastated places, Birch is held as sacred and has also been called the "mother tree," representing fertility and the feminine ability to give birth to what is yet to come. She is a caretaker and originator, not only by being first, but in two other key ways, which are: what it means to originate from Source and the energy of new beginnings.

What does it mean to originate from Source? Think of the whole Earth as a conscious being who holds a dream or a vision. Then imagine that the Earth's dream or vision is expressed through all of the elements and creatures including plants, animals, and humans. When you take the combination of consciousness and matter, that is the originating force of the birth of all beings. Birch helps you work with or know your origins be it your family of origin, ancestry, lineage, and other connections to Source so that you can know where you come from. This helps inform who you are on a deep soul level and the subsequent embodiment of your true nature. If you are curious about your origins, or want to explore the ancestral wounds and strengths you hold in your bones and being, Birch will accompany you on this journey and equip you with the safety and protection you may require to uncover the truth of who you are.

As an initiator, Birch's spirit is also one of beginnings, firsts, or starting something new and she is not afraid to leap in without knowing what the end result will be. The spirit of Birch helps you trust fully in yourself and your purpose so that the only safety net required is to do what you're here to do. If you aren't sure what that is, as you get to know Birch, she will initiate you, and your consciousness, into the evolutionary role you are here to play. She will help you bring all that you are into the world, including any gifts, skills, or medicine you have growing within you. Birch tends to these parts of you, and illuminates them, so that they may shine through.

If you are someone who avoids starting anything new, venturing into the unknown, or are afraid you can't do something that you've never tried (especially if you've always wanted to do it), Birch will support you as you take the first steps, and will encourage you to keep trying until the new thing feels natural. As you begin your own personal evolution, you also contribute to the evolution of the whole collective.

Birch empowers you to be a leader in your own life so that you may also light the way for others to find their own ability to lead as well. Light begets light, and whether it's a guiding force through darkness, or the flicker of energy that it takes to ignite something new, Birch generates the first spark then holds the light while you find your way through. She is a strong ally to call on and work with if you feel disempowered, like you have no choices, are waiting for others to start your life for you, or if you extinguish your own light (or that of those around you) to try to gain a sense of control. Birch will help you refuel, renew, and launch again and again with a deeper connection to your own inner light, energy, and purpose.

OVERVIEW OF BIRCH MEDICINE

P art of Birch's medicine has to do with being aware of treating yourself and others with care and respect. Before you take anything from Birch, be sure to ask her for permission to do so. Peeling away too much of her bark, especially if it's a ring of bark around the entire trunk, can damage or kill a Birch tree as her lifelines and sap run up and down her trunk. It's best to take a very small amount, moving vertically, or gather bark from a tree that has already fallen. Always take no more than you need for personal use.

As most parts of Birch are edible, there are many ways to work with her medicine. All varieties of Birch hold similar properties, though they will be slightly different based on the kind of tree, energy, and environment. In general, you can make a tea or infusion from her live twigs, fresh or dried leaves, and catkins. To test if a twig is alive, see if it bends. If it is brittle then it's dead and the medicine is gone too. Check the twigs to make sure they don't have any buds or new growth and, if they do, don't take too much. You only need a few leaves and a small twig or two to make a potent tea. Once you have what you need, steep in boiled water (cover the cup or jar so the nutrients don't escape on the steam) for at least twenty minutes before straining. You can also leave the infusion to sit for four hours, and then use externally as a poultice on wet eczema, rashes, or wounds. Another way to do this is to decoct the twigs or inner bark on the stovetop by placing them in water, bring to a boil, and then simmer for twenty minutes (also covered).

Birch also works well as a tincture by placing her bark, twigs broken into pieces, leaves and/or catkins in a jar of alcohol or apple cider vinegar for 4-6 weeks, then straining. For fresh Birch you can fill the jar and then cover with alcohol or vinegar, for dried, work with a ratio of approximately 1:5 Birch to liquid. A standard tincture dosage is about 30-60 drops in a cup or so of water. The tincture of Birch bark in particular works as an osteoblastic, meaning she helps build bone material and can offset conditions like osteoporosis, or aid in healing a broken bone, once set.

As an astringent, Birch tones and tightens throughout your entire system. This tonifying action helps your body work more efficiently and, at the same time, fortifies and heals areas of weakness, and reduces fluid retention. Birch has an affinity for the urinary tract and kidneys, treating infections, and increasing the production and flow of urine to help move waste, gravel, disease, and discomfort out of the body. With a bitter quality, drinking Birch aids in digestion, protects the liver, and her twigs and bark work well as an anti-inflammatory and analgesic to heal, repair, and bring pain relief to the overall body. This relief may be for acute conditions, or longer-term, chronic pain such as arthritis and aching joints. She also helps boost your immune system and is anti-viral. Just as Birch's lifeline is her sap, she helps your "sap" run efficiently throughout your body by boosting blood flow through toned and tightened veins, increasing circulation, while also reducing cholesterol. She even helps manage your insulin levels.

Birch water or sap itself is also potent with rich medicine, considered a cleansing spring tonic to promote overall health and get your juices flowing after winter. There are a few ways to respectfully tap a Birch tree. Before you start, again, ask permission to do so and choose a tree that has good access to everything she needs (rich soil, sun, and water) as a healthy tree will be more likely to recover from any intrusion. To collect her sap or water, you can either carefully drill a hole a few inches into the trunk, insert a natural spout like a piece of wood made into a tube, and then guide the fluid into a container. Drilling a hole can introduce a gateway for infection, which can ultimately kill the tree, so be sure that this action is in right alignment for both you and Birch. To be less invasive, you might use a knife instead of a drill or, for even less impact on the tree herself, break a small branch and attach a bottle to where you broke it off to receive the sap.

Birch water or sap is clear and has a slightly sweet flavor. The sap is nutrient rich and contains vitamin B3, C, antioxidants, manganese and magnesium, and aids in strengthening and developing your bones, protecting you from cell damage, and also aids in digestion. Plus, it's refreshing and cooling.

Since Birch tightens and tones, she helps your skin look and feel radiant, and her medicine is becoming increasingly popular in skin care products. Birch shrinks cellulite and reduces sun damage to the skin (including treating or reversing potentially cancerous skin growth related to exposure). You can make an oil from Birch too, for topical use, by picking fresh, healthy leaves, and placing them in a jar, covering them with oil and letting them sit for four-to-six weeks, then straining. Along with aiding in toning skin, Birch brings relief to sore, aching muscles and you can rub the oil directly on your body or make a salve. To do this, place about half an ounce of beeswax to four ounces of Birch oil in a jar. Place the jar, uncovered, inside a pot on the stovetop with a few inches of water and then bring to a medium heat where you can watch the wax melt. Once melted, either leave to cool and use the jar as your container or pour into smaller jars or metal containers for future use.

Birch herself, with her white bark and black lines and knots, looks like bones. As a foundational tree on the Earth, it makes sense that she also helps nourish and reset the bones of the humans and animals who live here as well. To strengthen, grow, and solidify that foundational structure around which the human body exists. Birch's medicine is also of knowing something in your bones. Be it intuition, inner guidance, or drawing upon the collective consciousness, Birch helps you feel into the structures within you so that you may call upon the wisdom that you carry. Perhaps this knowledge has been carried through the bones of your ancestors, all the way back to when Birch originated here in this place.

BIRCH FOLKLORE

Birch has many folk or common names including The White Goddess, The Lady of the Woods, The Silver Maiden, and The Birchen Maiden indicating her regal status and association with the divine feminine. Associated with fertility, love, and protection, Birch shares connections with powerful female goddesses including the Norse Goddess Freya, Venus in Ancient Rome, Brigid in Celtic traditions, and Blodeuwedd in Wales. Each of these goddesses, in their own way champion birth, rebirth, new beginnings, blossoming and nurturing oneself (and others) as well as acting from fierce love, especially when in defense of women's freedom of choice, protection of hearth, home, lovers, and children. Celebrated in spring festivals such as Bealtaine (or Beltane), Easter, and May Day, Birch's green leaves appear early in the season, marking the end of winter and the stirring of new life.

Birch's reputation in Britain as the oldest tree holds her in high regard by humans and she is viewed as the Cosmic World Tree in Latvian, Northern Asian,

Siberian, Mongolian, and Turkic folk beliefs.[1] The world tree represents the connection between all of the worlds—the heavens, sky world, or "as above," the material earth plane of daily life and physical being, and the underworld, or "so below." While standing between all of these worlds, Birch, is known as a sky ladder, and provides access to the world of the gods, spirits, and ascended masters or ancestors; all that is "above" and exists in the elements of air and ether.

To access this world with Birch, you can enter an altered state of consciousness, or trance-state, through meditation, a drum journey, or by sitting with Birch and merging with her. Then, with the desire to travel to the "as above," imagine you are moving up Birch's trunk and into her branches. When you're ready, you can launch yourself into the air and fly through the sky. Some experience this as active imagination, while for others it's as though your consciousness leaves your body and travels through the sky both separate from and connected to your body.

A journey is often done with a specific intention, or as a quest to gain information, so it's helpful to distill your reason for traveling down to a few words and then repeat it three times before beginning your journey. For example, you may say something like, "my intention is to meet a spirit guide." As you journey, you enter into a dream-like state where you're not quite awake or asleep, and the intention shapes or forms what happens along the way. As you travel, with an intention to meet your spirit guide, for example, you can ask any beings you meet along the way if they are your guide. You may be a visual person and see images, or you may receive sensations in your body, movements, hear sounds, or a knowing of this information in another way. If you start with a different intention, that will, in turn, shape the journey that unfolds. Whatever your intention or experience, when you return to your body at the conclusion of your journey through the "as above," be sure to write down, draw, or integrate whatever information comes through so that you can bring it back down to Earth.

Birch is the first letter, "B," (pronounced Beith, meaning Birch) in the first Celtic written alphabet and language called the Ogham. There is an entire set of twenty characters in the Ogham which are sounds of and representation of trees. The human and plant worlds at this time were so integrated that the trees themselves were what made up the first written language and way of communicating and are, still, the basis of all of the human language that grew out of that system into Gaelic and Irish tongues. With this power of being an originating human language, Birch helps you discern what truly needs to be communicated, when, and how to do so. Each of the Ogham letters or symbols also is also used in a system of divination. In this system, the symbols are inscribed upon or carved into pieces of wood or rock and, much like Viking Runes, are either pulled out of a bag or cast upon the ground while asking a question or stating an intention.

In modern times there are also Ogham decks of cards similar to the Tarot with the trees drawn on each one. When you look at the symbols or card(s) that have been pulled, from the meaning of the tree behind each representation, you can discern information or knowing about the question you have asked. In this system of divination, Birch represents new beginnings and will help clear the path for you to start something new.[2] When you pull the Birch Ogham, be ready to start something, be it a project, moving somewhere new, a job, a relationship or partnership, or call on her energy when you want assistance with a new endeavor, way of life, or when parts of you are calling for rebirth.

The Ogham has yet another important meaning related to the calendar, wheel of the year, somewhat similar to astrology although not related to the planetary influences but each of the thirteen segments of the year or lunar months are associated with a tree. Birch governs the time from December 24th through January 20th and supports the energy of the winter solstice and new year. In this system of tree astrology, people born during the month of Birch will have qualities of "the achiever," may have a new or different outlook on life than most, are ambitious leaders who strive to expand their knowledge, move through uncharted territory, and encourage other people along their path through sharing what they have to offer. They are often seen as charming and bright.[3]

Birch's association with the written language isn't exclusive to the British Isles. Some of the oldest Buddhist texts from the first century are written on Birch, as are many ancient Sanskrit, and Russian texts.[4] Many speculate that the name Birch comes from the Sanskrit word bhurga, which means "a tree whose bark is used for writing upon."[5] In North America, Birch also played a crucial role in language and writing down knowledge. In the Ojibwe language, wilgwaasaback means birch bark scroll (or wilgwaasabakoon for multiple scrolls).[6] Upon these scrolls the Anishnaabe people wrote or etched a series of symbols: knowledge to be passed to future generations including rituals, maps, history, teachings, skills, and also used them for ceremony.[7] These scrolls were sometimes shared or sometimes they were hidden in caves or buried in the ground. Paper Birch (*Betula papyrifera*) also serves to make canoes for travel to new places, migration, hunting, or recreation.

Birch are traditionally made into besom brooms (a kind of broom made by tying a bundle of twigs to a branch) for cleansing and sweeping out both the physical dirt and energetic debris from a home. Branches of Birch are also used to "beat the bounds," an ancient custom across Britain and New England where a group of people walk around the boundary of a township, parish, or land waving a stick of Birch. This ritual created energetic protection, renewed each time it was done, and also helped drive out or clear stagnant energy from the land, aiding in its renewal and also protecting all who lived within the bounds. Cradles made from Birch were said to protect the baby within from psychic harm and kidnapping by the fairies. Make a wand from Birch to create protection around you or others.

Through her association with new beginnings, the evolution of consciousness, and being a conduit for creating and preserving knowledge, Birch leads the way for each new generation. She holds the past, is open to the present, and helps bridge new pathways of what the future will be. The future is fluid, and Birch knows how to navigate between what we, collectively, need to hold onto from the past and what needs to be thrown out, reimagined, and born in new ways. She can help you discern the same in your own life, too.

JOURNEY INTO THE DREAM WITH BIRCH

Another way to work with the spirit of Birch is to call on her wherever you are, even if you aren't physically with the tree. Her energy and consciousness are everywhere, and you can dream with her, feel her presence, or ask for her help, wherever you are. To aid in this, let's take a guided journey with Birch and see what happens.

You might want to take a few moments before reading on to center yourself. If you'd like to, find a comfortable way to sit or lay down. Close your eyes if that feels safe or let them be soft. Take a few breaths and allow yourself to feel your body around the breath. When you feel at ease, open your eyes and read this bedtime story with a soft dreamy feeling.

You're cozy in your bed, about to go to sleep, when you see a glowing golden door appear in front of you. As you move toward the door, it opens, and you step through and find yourself standing in a barren land of craggy rock covered with ice, as far as you can see. To your left there's a frozen ocean filled with sharp icebergs. You can feel the cold of the ground underneath your feet and, as you look down, the ice around your feet melts from the warmth of your body.

You start to venture into this new land, creating melted footprints with every step you take. Notice how you feel in this place.

You look up at the cloud-covered sky, and you can see the silhouette of the sun, hiding behind the grey-white. The clouds start to move across the sky. Slowly at first and then with more speed. They start to move towards you, coming closer, until you stand at the bottom of a staircase made out of clouds.

You take the first step, and then the next. Moving higher and higher up into the sky. Moving through layers of air. Notice how you feel.

As you reach the top of the staircase, there's a white, puffy cloud waiting for you. You sit on the cloud and it travels, with you safely on it, across the sky. You float through the air with freedom and ease.

In the distance you see a gigantic golden light. The glow pulls you toward it and, as you arrive, you see a floating forest of Birch trees. The trees are white and silver, stretching up further into the sky, their leaves making a dome of gold. You step off of your cloud and explore this forest in the sky. You can hear the trees whispering to one another.

One tree calls you to her and you approach, placing your hands on her trunk. She invites you to climb up into her branches. You climb up, finding the perfect branch to sit in. Allow yourself to be held by the Birch tree.

As you sit, the golden leaves start to vibrate and shiver around you. Then, you notice that each leaf has an ancient symbol inscribed upon it. You are surrounded by an ancient language. You reach up and take the leaf closest to you, holding it in your hands.

When you look at the leaf, you see a shape or a symbol.

Ask this shape or symbol what it means. Receive an answer.

The leaf glows brighter and brighter and, as you keep watching, the symbol disappears and is replaced with a word or an image that shows you where you come from.

See where you come from clearly.

Ask any questions you may have. See the answers appear on the leaf.

Then, with this knowledge, now ask what you need to start in your life. What needs to happen next. Receive the answers that come.

A scroll of Birch bark appears beside you, with all of the answers you need recorded upon it. You take the scroll, then look at it, feel what's written. Keep this scroll with you as you climb back down the tree, giving thanks for all that was given.

You ask Birch what you can do for her. Receive whatever answer comes.

Walk back through the floating forest of shimmering Birch. Feel the energy here.

Keeping the knowledge you have received with you, step back onto your cloud and sit or lay down as the cloud takes you across the expansive sky. Notice how you move through space and time.

The cloud arrives at the top of the stairs and you walk back down through the sky. Each step disappears behind you as you descend. Back down to the land.

The land now, transformed. The ice has melted, and all around you see plants and trees. Notice any creatures or beings moving around you. The land is luscious, vibrant, beautiful. Feel the beauty around you.

You navigate through the land with ease, returning to the golden door from which you came. The door opens and you step through the threshold, coming back into your body and back into your breath, bringing all the knowledge you received back with you.

Once you are back fully from this dreamy journey, you might write down feelings that emerged, any information about where you come from, what you need to start, what you will do for Birch, or continue dreaming in some way.

A BONUS BENEFIT

One of the most valuable parts of any practice where you are working with trees and in the worlds of consciousness is developing trust. You might be someone to discount or not trust in your own intuition. Likely because of messages you have received from a culture that holds value in beliefs of power, dominance, and separation and/or early childhood messaging that was reinforced over time. For example, if you were open to the trees as a kid, an adult who was already closed off may have told you that your experience was invalid or not real. While this was not true, someone you may have loved or who was in a position of authority dismissed your experience. This messaging often damages your relationship to your own intuition and eventually causes an imbalance when it comes to trusting your instincts (especially when it comes to psychic awareness or abilities).

Beginning the process of being with and merging with trees and their world helps to heal this split. In time, and with repetition, it can help you reconnect to your own psychic and spiritual gifts and self. This, in turn, can empower you to feel more whole, connected, and become able to make more decisions from a place of safety and trust in yourself. As you continue to grow in these ways, you can go into a dream-like space or vast field of consciousness and bring back visions, dreams, or instruction on what to do in this physical realm of your daily life and personal growth.

OVER TO YOU

Some may say that plant spirit healing works on the psychological level because we are able to see a mirror into ourselves through them. Others call it intuition or a psychic awareness and receive all kinds of different information. Whatever words work for you, there is no harm in seeing what might come from connecting with a plant or tree. You can even ask to see what would be for the greater good of all, if that helps. The most important thing is that you find your own direct relationship with Birch and discover for yourself what you can give to one another.

You were called to this short book for some reason. Whether it was to know more about tree spirit medicine, Birch, your origins, evolutionary path, something you need to start, or for some other reason, perhaps unknown, Birch called you here with her magic. Now you are equipped to venture out and travel between worlds, dream with Birch, and see what transformation comes. Transformation and healing aren't always easy and may not feel comfortable at times, but with a strong ally like Birch, and your own intuition and guidance, I hope you will continue to explore your relationship with her and with the plant world.

ACKNOWLEDGEMENTS

First, I'd like to thank my dear friend and editor, Deanna McFadden, for her constant support, curiosity, and skillful editorial hand. While writing this book I reflected fondly on my first experience with merging in general, led by Susan Grimaldi at the New England Women's Herbal Conference. This was followed by a Shamanic Weed Walk with Susun Weed where she helped participants be with and merge with plants. Since then I have also worked with Elyse Pomeranz who brought in the option of painting or drawing with the consciousness of the plants and am so grateful to have completed a three-year apprenticeship in Sacred Plant Medicine with Carole Guyett in Ireland where I learned to go even deeper into the dream. Each of these teachers has taught me how to enter the plant world and to walk between that world, the dream world, and our human one. To understand that they aren't separate but feed one another and need tending. It is from this place of deep gratitude that I wish to now share these practices with you in my own voice and way. Of course, with the deepest respect and love for the plants who are guiding it all.

ENDNOTES

[1] http://folklore.ee/folklore/vol16/oak2.pdf

[2] https://oghamdivination.wordpress.com/ogham-alphabet/birch/

[3] https://blog.fantasticgardeners.co.uk/whats-your-tree-sign-according-to-celtic-tree-astrology/

[4] https://en.wikipedia.org/wiki/Birch_bark_manuscript

[5] https://treesforlife.org.uk/into-the-forest/trees-plants-animals/trees/birch/birch-mythology-and-folklore/

[6] https://en.wikipedia.org/wiki/Wiigwaasabak

[7] https://www.youtube.com/watch?v=lfSB4uyhMUk

ABOUT THE AUTHOR

Heather Sanderson has been working with plant spirits her whole life. In 2013 she studied herbal medicine at Third Root in Brooklyn, NY which led her to a 3-year Sacred Plant Medicine Apprenticeship with Carole Guyett in County Clare, Ireland. It was through this training, and several initiations with plants, that she became immersed in the dream and consciousness of the plant world and found a passion to share it with others. For more information visit www.journeythroughyoga.com.

BOOKS BY THIS AUTHOR

Plant Spirit Short Reads
Dreaming with Dandelion
Dreaming with Elder
Dreaming with Heather
Dreaming with Holly
Dreaming with Goldenrod
Dreaming with Lavender
Dreaming with Nettle
Dreaming with Red Clover
Dreaming with Rhubarb
Dreaming with Rosemary
Dreaming with Sumac
Dreaming with Sunflower
Dreaming with Trillium
Dreaming with Violet

Tree Spirit Short Reads
Dreaming with Apple
Dreaming with Birch
Dreaming with Hawthorn
Dreaming with Oak
Dreaming with Redwood
Dreaming with Spruce
Dreaming with Willow

Healing Arts Short Reads
Loving Kindness for Everyday Life
Understanding Reiki
Yoga Nidra for Everyday Life

Poetry
Sister, (a collection of poems)

The Future is Possible Series
Building the Future Now Through Reiki: A Conversation with Nathalie Biermanns
Building the Future Now Through Yoga: A Conversation with Deanna Green
Creative Being: A Conversation with Gérome Barry
Envisioning New Ecosystems: A Conversation with Stewart Hoyt
Holding Space to Heal: A Conversation with Holly Ramey
Nature Sanctuary for the Future: A Conversation with Marina Levitina
What Art Can Do: A Conversation with Janet Morgan

Visit www.majesticwisdompublishing.com to learn more.

Made in the USA
Columbia, SC
12 January 2025